EASY GUITAR
WITH NOTES & TAB

the best of
mercyme

T0065940

Cover photo by David Molnar

ISBN 978-1-4803-8300-5

HAL•LEONARD®
CORPORATION
7777 W. BLUEMOUND RD. P.O. BOX 13819 MILWAUKEE, WI 53213

Visit Hal Leonard Online at
www.halleonard.com

STRUM AND PICK PATTERNS

This chart contains the suggested strum and pick patterns that are referred to by number at the beginning of each song in this book. The symbols ⊓ and ∨ in the strum patterns refer to down and up strokes, respectively. The letters in the pick patterns indicate which right-hand fingers play which strings.

p = thumb
i = index finger
m = middle finger
a = ring finger

For example; Pick Pattern 2
is played: thumb - index - middle - ring

Strum Patterns   Pick Patterns

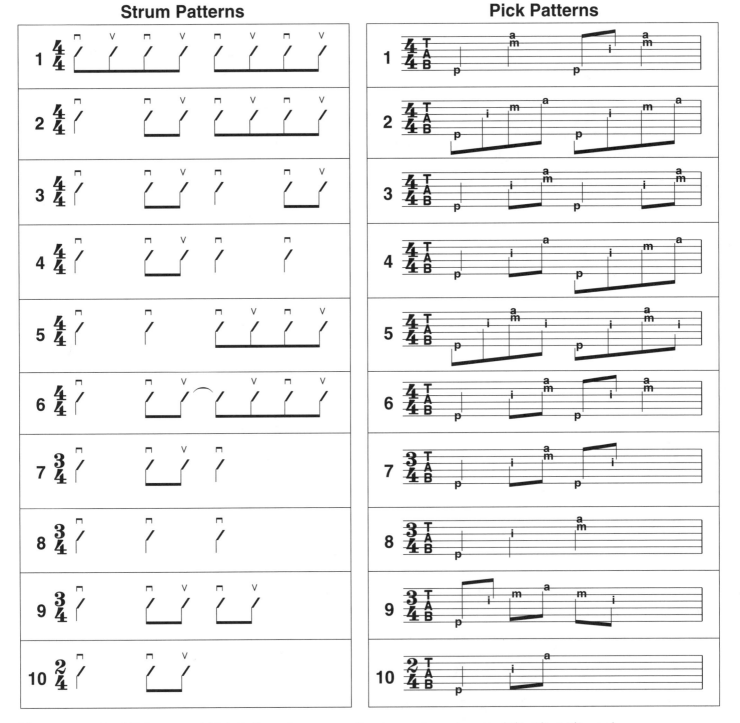

You can use the 3/4 Strum and Pick Patterns in songs written in compound meter (6/8, 9/8, 12/8, etc.).
For example, you can accompany a song in 6/8 by playing the 3/4 pattern twice in each measure.
The 4/4 Strum and Pick Patterns can be used for songs written in cut time (¢) by doubling the note time values in the patterns. Each pattern would therefore last two measures in cut time.

Finally Home

Words and Music by Bart Millard, Barry Graul and Mike Scheuchzer

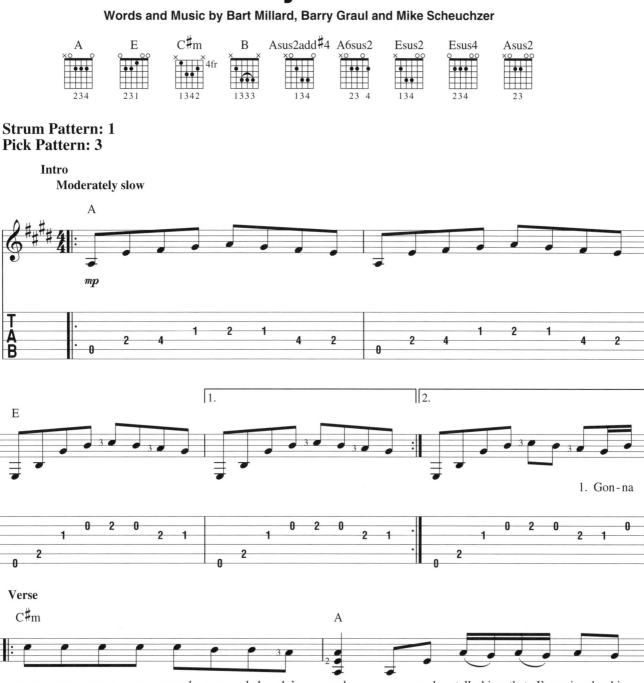

Strum Pattern: 1
Pick Pattern: 3

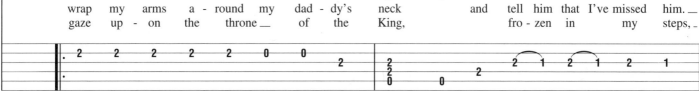

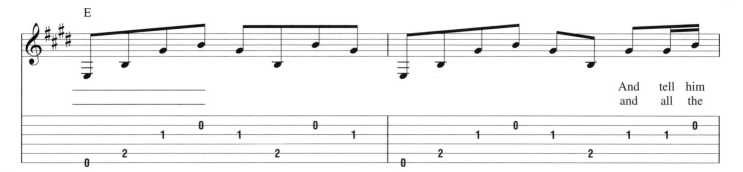

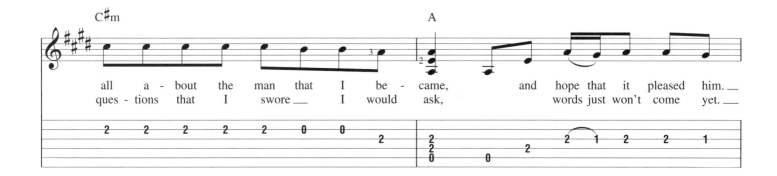

all a-bout the man that I be-came, and hope that it pleased him. ___
ques-tions that I swore ___ I would ask, words just won't come yet. ___

There's so much I wan-na say, so
I'm so a-mazed at what I've seen, so much

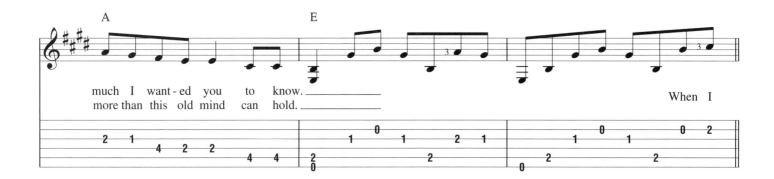

much I want-ed you to know. _____
more than this old mind can hold. _____

When I

𝄋 Chorus

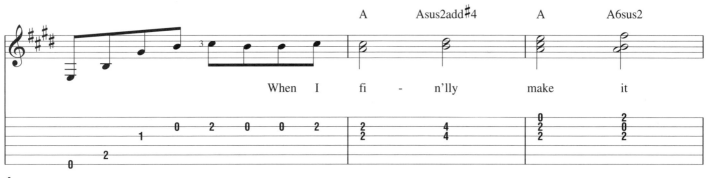

fi - n'lly make it home.

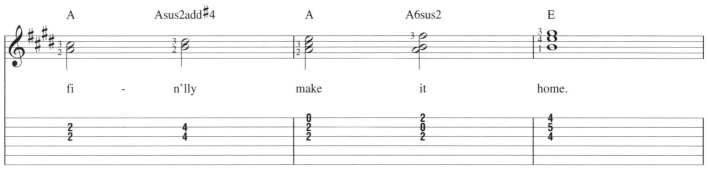

When I fi - n'lly make it

home.
2. Then I'll
And the

Bridge

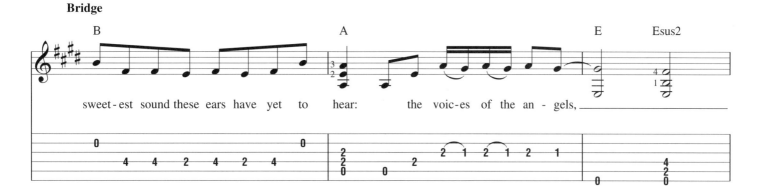

sweet-est sound these ears have yet to hear: the voic-es of the an - gels,

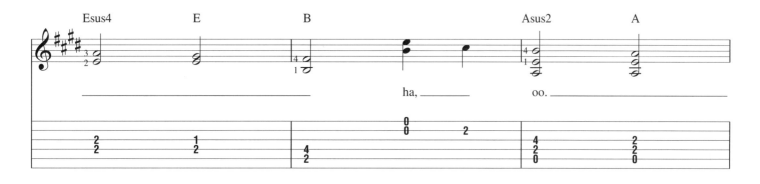

ha, oo.

D.S. al Coda

Coda

When I

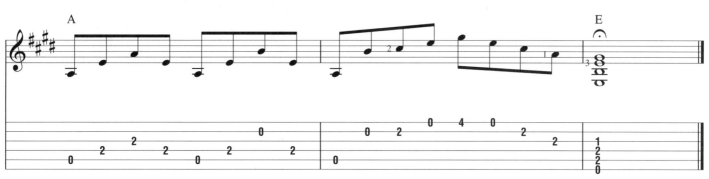

All of Creation

Words and Music by MercyMe, Dan Muckala and Brown Bannister

*Capo III

Strum Pattern: 5
Pick Pattern: 5

*Optional: To match recording, place capo at 3rd fret.

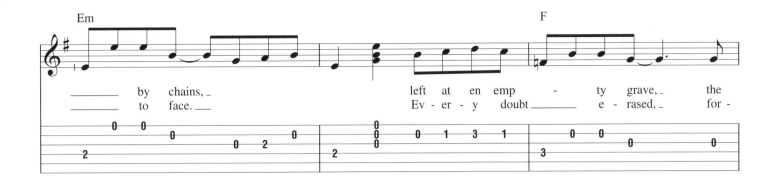

_____ by chains,_ left at en emp - - ty grave,_ the_
_____ to face._ Ev - er - y doubt_____ e - rased,_ for -_

_sin - ner and the sa - cred re - solved.__
_ev - er we will wor - ship the King.__

Chorus

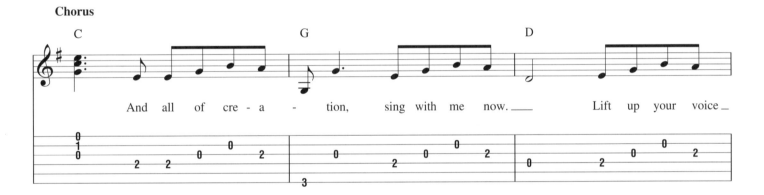

_And all of cre - a - - tion, sing with me now. __ Lift up your voice__

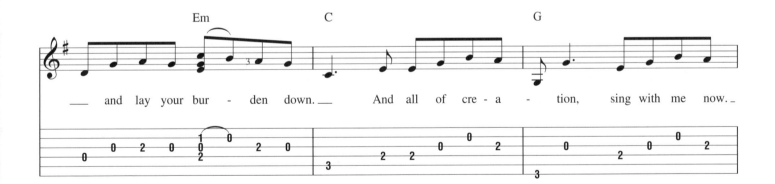

___ and lay your bur - den down._ And all of cre - a - - tion, sing with me now._

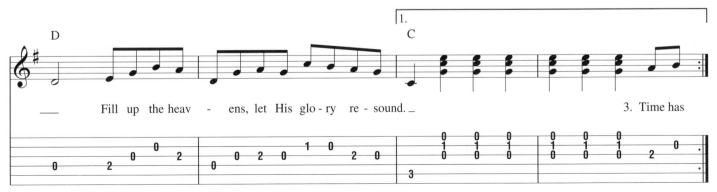

1.

___ Fill up the heav - - ens, let His glo - ry re - sound._ 3. Time has_

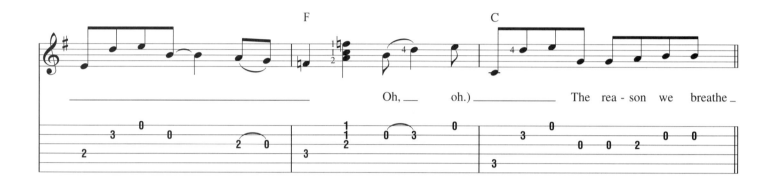

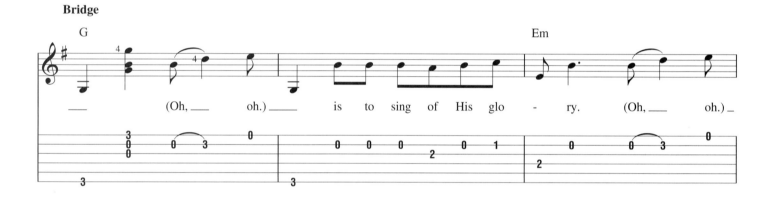

Bridge

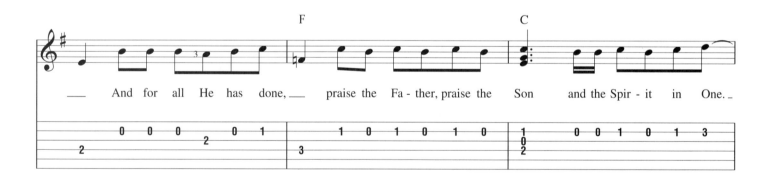

Chorus

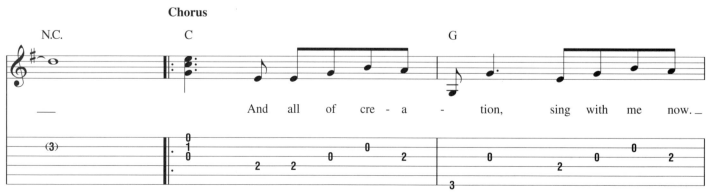

Lift up your voice ___ and lay your bur - den down. ___ And all of cre - a -

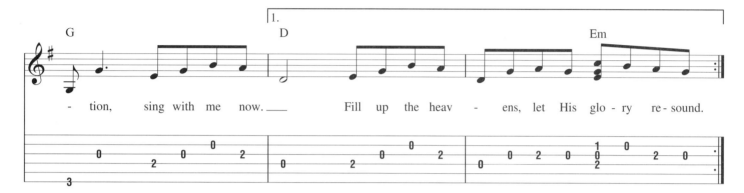

- tion, sing with me now. ___ Fill up the heav - ens, let His glo - ry re - sound.

___ Let His glo - ry re - sound. ___ (Oh, ___ oh.) ___

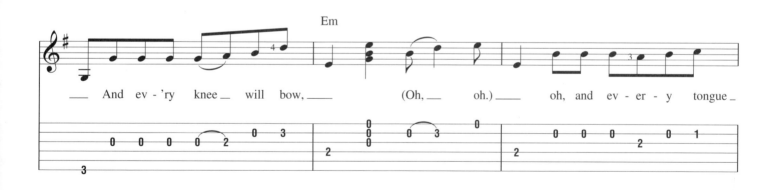

___ And ev - 'ry knee ___ will bow, ___ (Oh, ___ oh.) ___ oh, and ev - er - y tongue ___

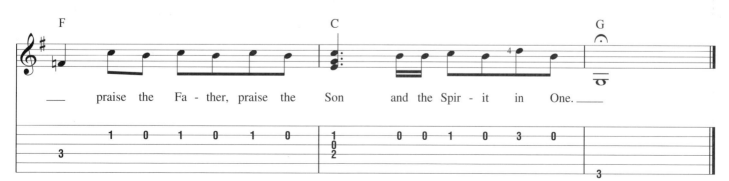

___ praise the Fa - ther, praise the Son and the Spir - it in One. ___

Bring the Rain

**Words and Music by Bart Millard, Barry Graul, Jim Bryson,
Nathan Cochran, Mike Scheuchzer and Robby Shaffer**

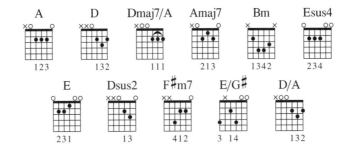

Strum Pattern: 4
Pick Pattern: 4

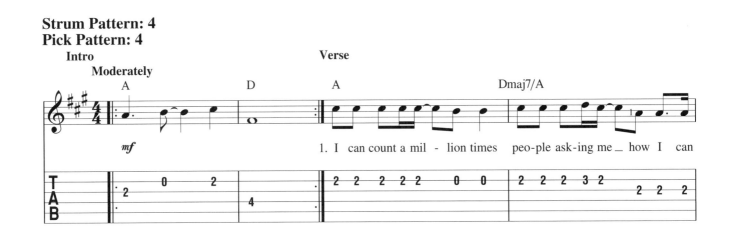

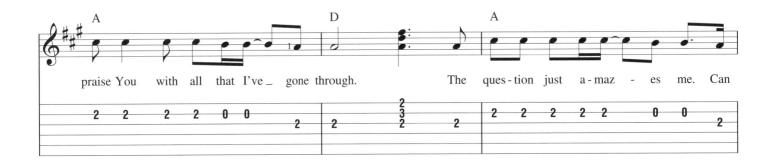

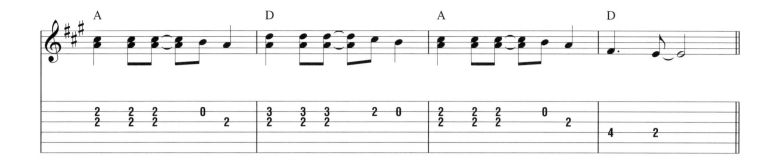

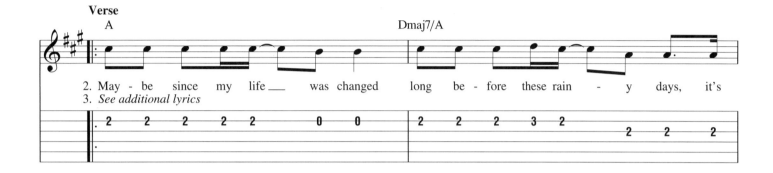

Verse

2. May - be since my life ___ was changed long be - fore these rain - y days, it's
3. *See additional lyrics*

nev - er real - ly ev - er crossed my mind to turn my back on You, ___ oh Lord, my

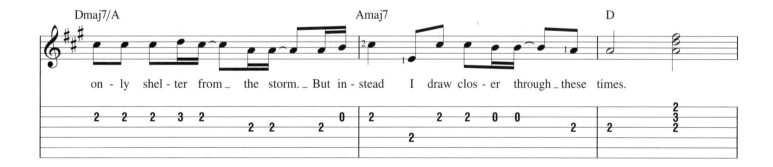

on - ly shel - ter from ___ the storm. ___ But in - stead I draw clos - er through ___ these times.

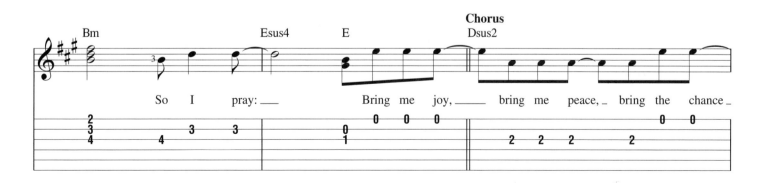

So I pray: ___ Bring me joy, ___ bring me peace, ___ bring the chance ___

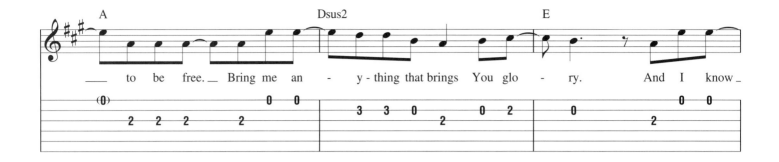

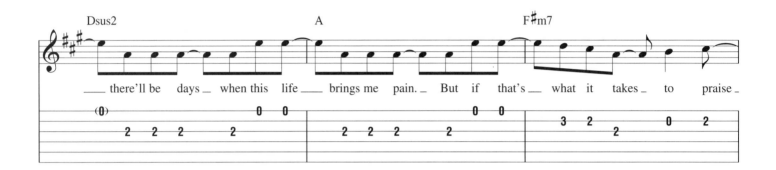

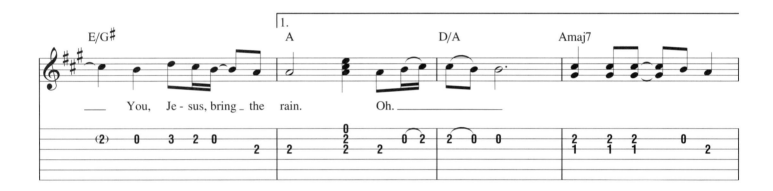

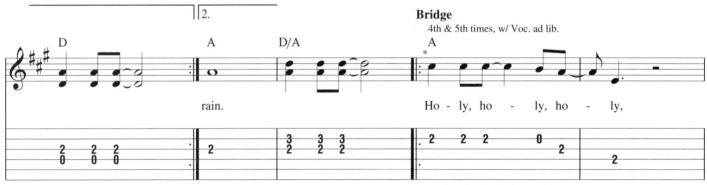

*1st time, let chords ring next 8 meas.

might - y. _____ And I for - ev - er sing. might - y.

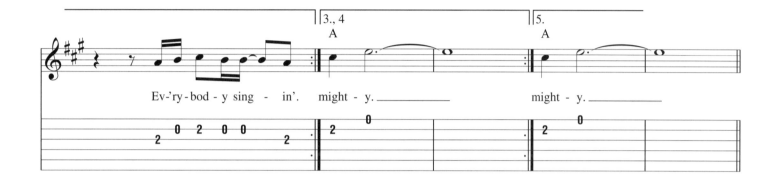

Ev-'ry-bod - y sing - in'. might - y. _____ might - y. _____

Outro

Ho - ly, ho - ly, ho - ly, ho - ly, ho - ly, ho - ly ___ is the Lord God Al -

*Let chords ring till end.

might - y, is the Lord ___ God Al - might - y.

Additional Lyrics

3. I am Yours regardless of the clouds that may loom above,
   Because You are much greater than my pain.
   You who made a way for me by suffering Your destiny.
   So tell me, what's a little rain?
   So I pray:

God with Us

Words and Music by Bart Millard, Nathan Cochran, Mike Scheuchzer, Jim Bryson, Barry Graul and Robby Shaffer

*Tune down 1/2 step
(low to high) Eb-Ab-Db-Gb-Bb-Eb

Strum Pattern: 1
Pick Pattern: 1

*Optional: To match recording, tune down 1/2 step.
**Down stroke

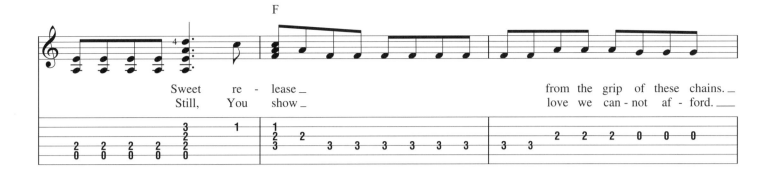

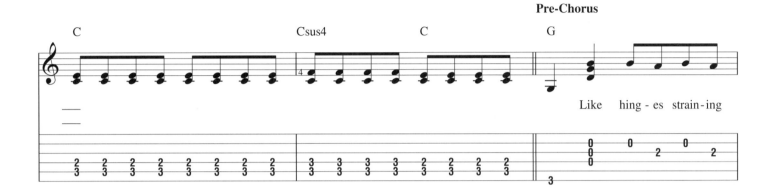

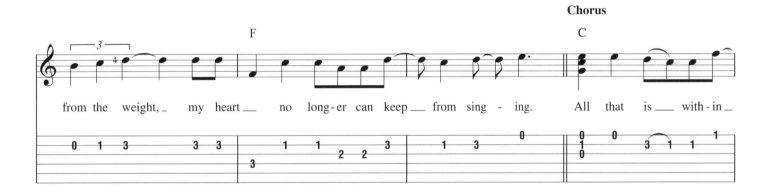

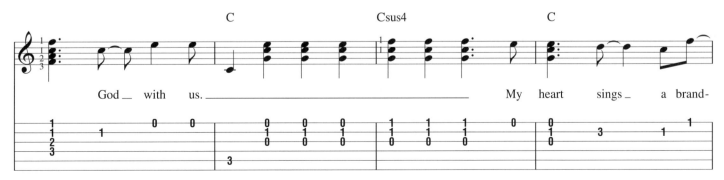

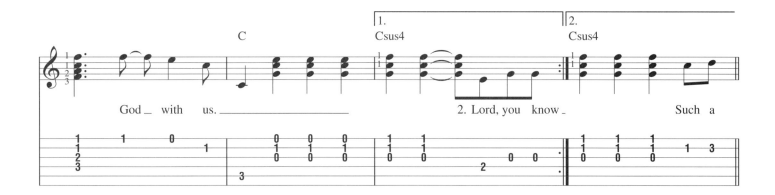

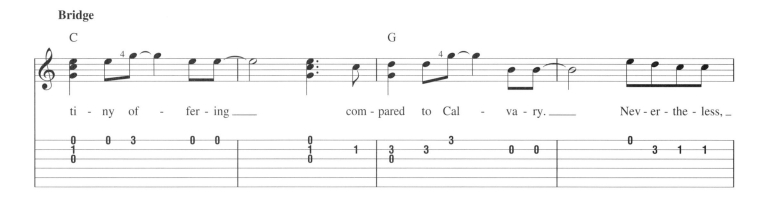

Bridge

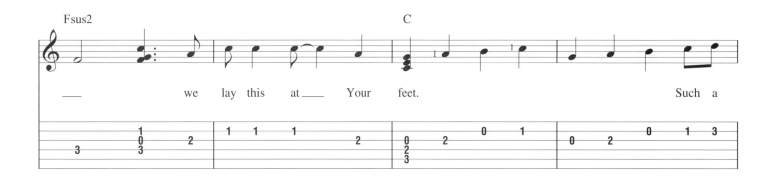

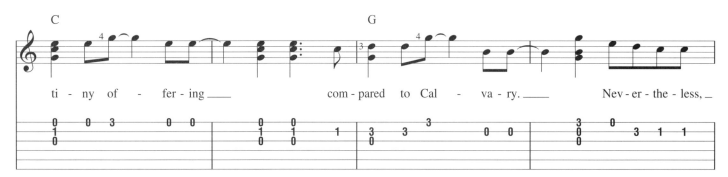

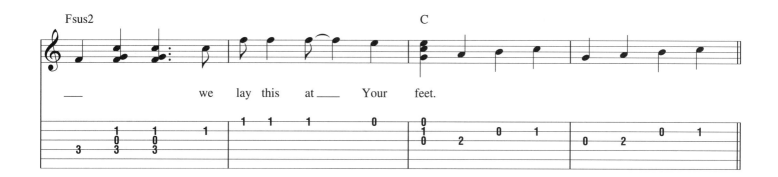

we lay this at ___ Your feet.

Outro-Chorus

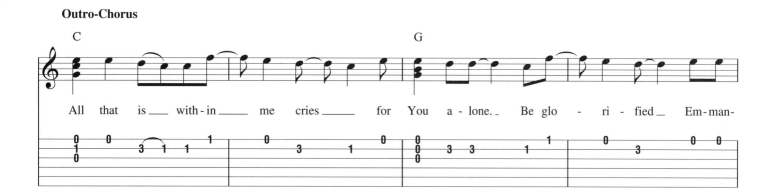

All that is ___ with-in ___ me cries ___ for You a - lone. ___ Be glo - ri - fied ___ Em - man-

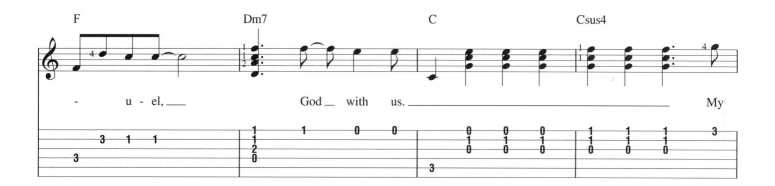

- u - el, ___ God ___ with us. _____ My

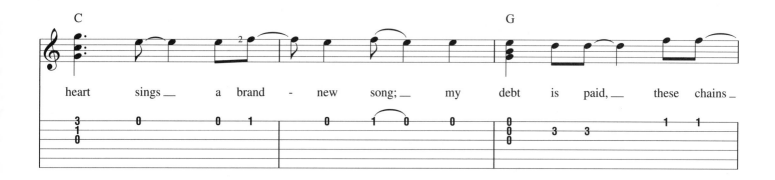

heart sings ___ a brand - new song; ___ my debt is paid, ___ these chains ___

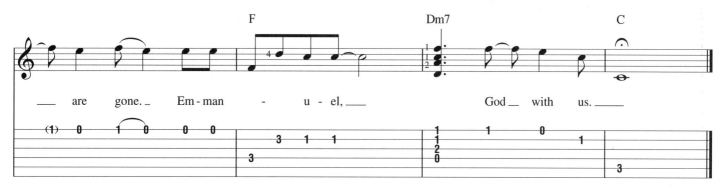

___ are gone. ___ Em - man - u - el, ___ God ___ with us.

Here with Me

Words and Music by Brad Russell, Bart Millard, Michael Scheuchzer, James Bryson, Robin Shaffer, Nathan Cochran, Barry Graul, Dan Muckala and Pete Kipley

Strum Pattern: 5
Pick Pattern: 1

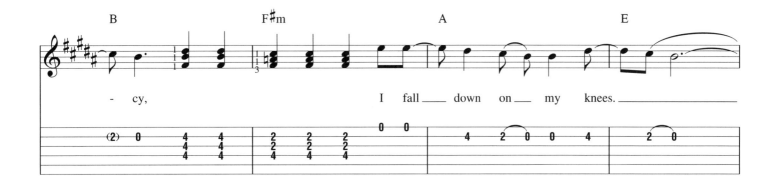

-cy, I fall ___ down on ___ my knees. ___

𝄋 Chorus

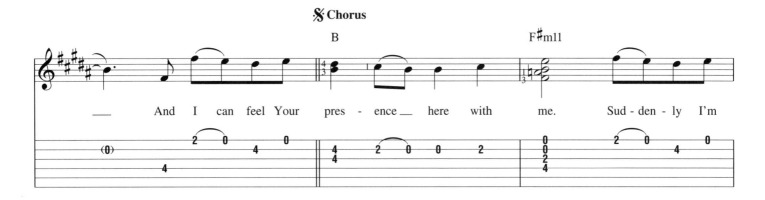

___ And I can feel Your pres - ence ___ here with me. Sud - den - ly I'm

lost with - in ___ Your beau - ty, caught up in the won - der ___ of Your

touch. Here in this mo - ment I ___ sur - ren - der to ___ Your

To Coda ⊕

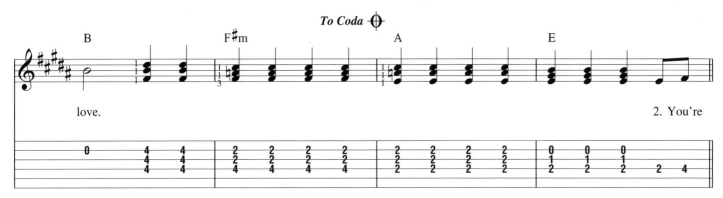

love. 2. You're

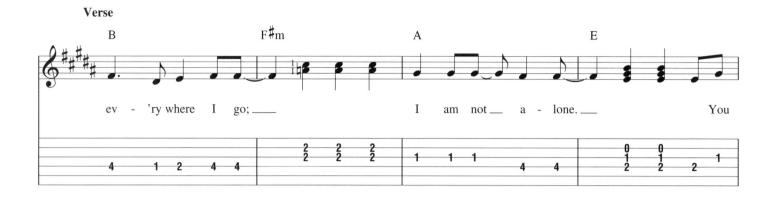

ev - 'ry where I go; ___   I am not ___ a - lone. ___   You

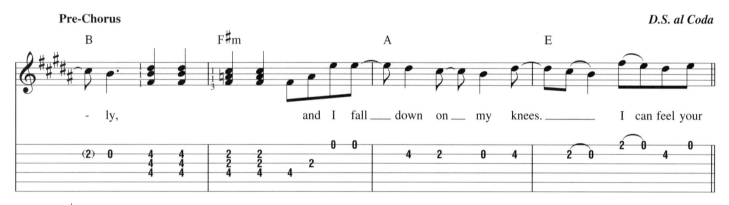

call me   as Your own, ___   to know You and ___ be   known. _   You are ho -

Pre-Chorus   *D.S. al Coda*

- ly,   and I fall ___ down on ___ my knees. _____ I can feel your

Coda

Bridge

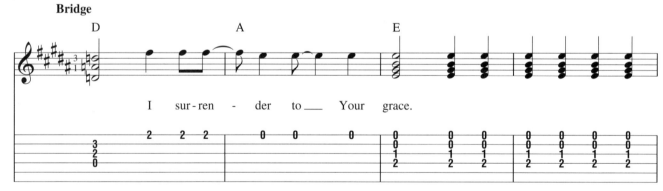

I sur - ren - der to ___ Your grace.

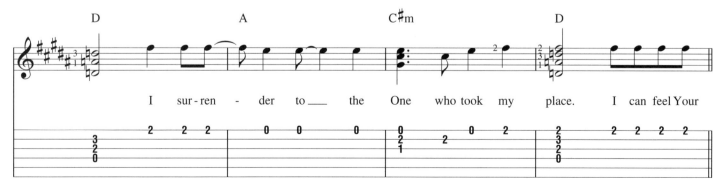

I sur - ren - der to ___ the One who took my   place. I can feel Your

Chorus

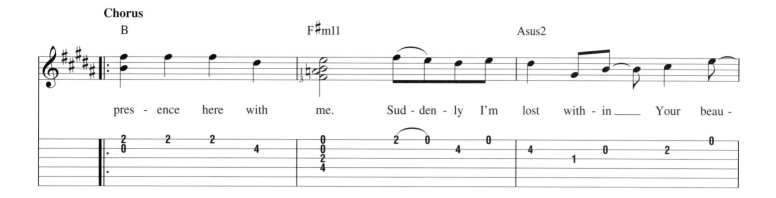

pres - ence here with me. Sud - den - ly I'm lost with - in _____ Your beau -

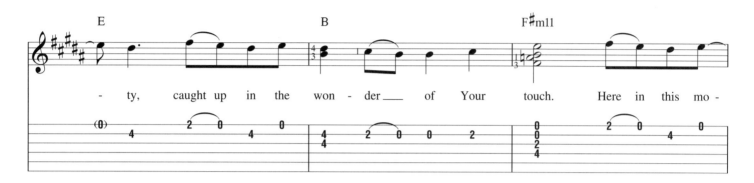

- ty, caught up in the won - der _____ of Your touch. Here in this mo -

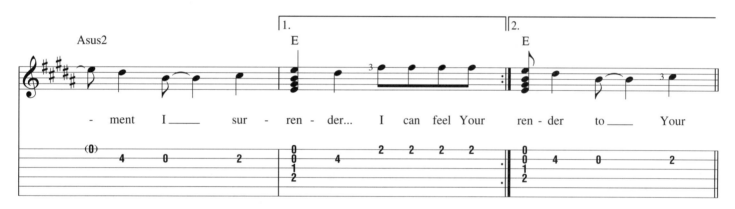

- ment I _____ sur - ren - der... I can feel Your ren - der to _____ Your

Outro

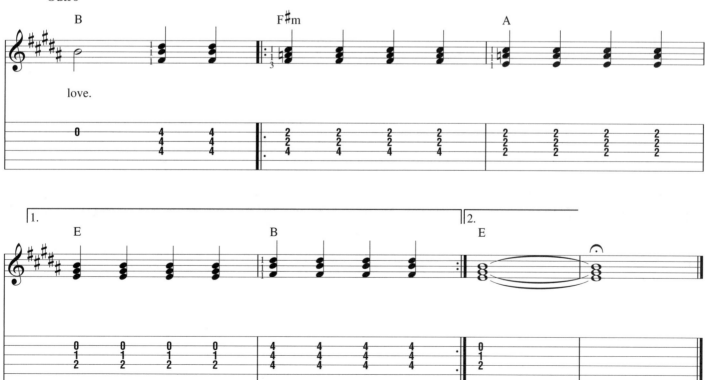

love.

Hold Fast

Words and Music by Bart Millard, Barry Graul, Jim Bryson, Nathan Cochran, Mike Scheuchzer and Robby Shaffer

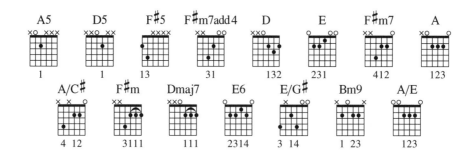

Strum Pattern: 1, 4
Pick Pattern: 4, 5

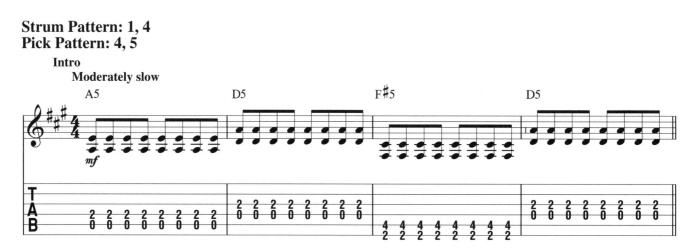

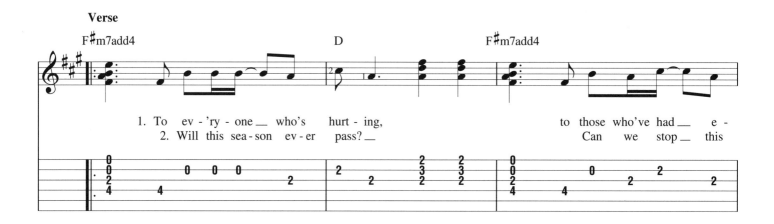

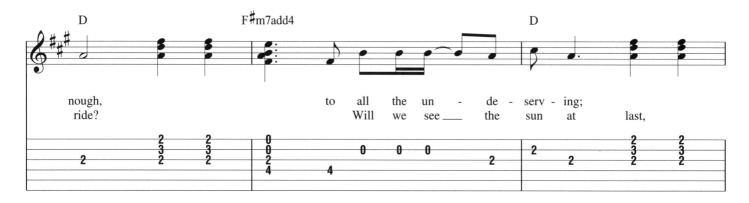

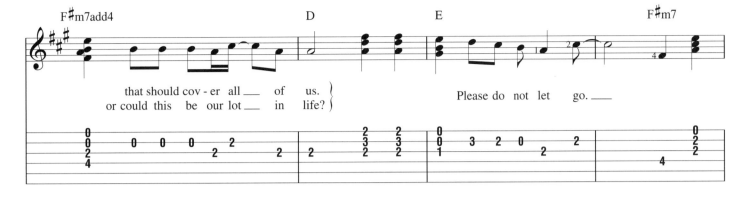

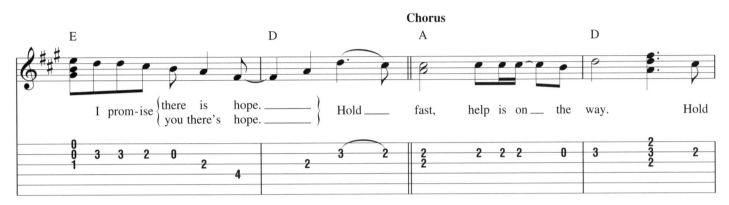

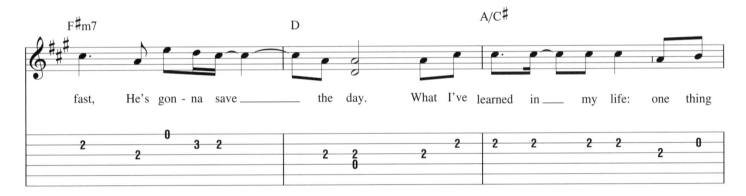

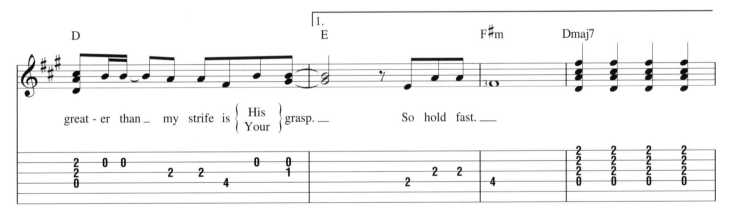

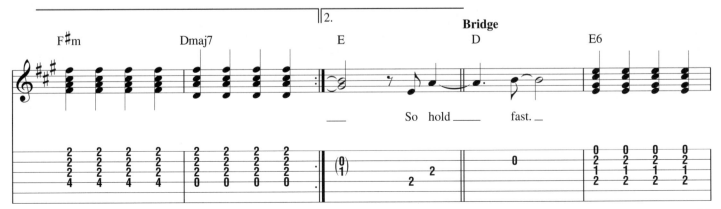

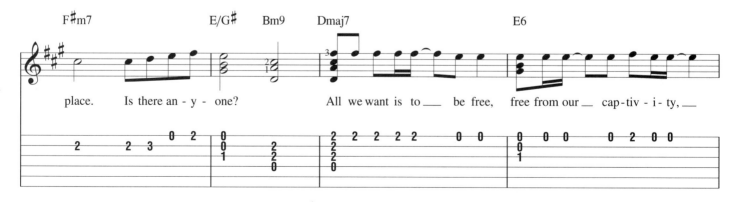

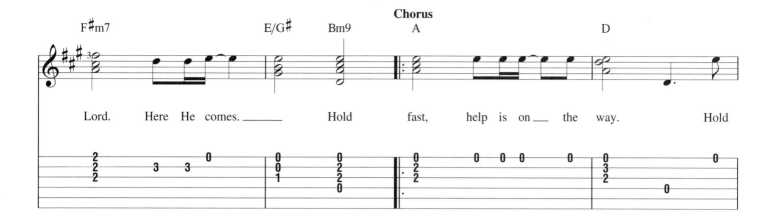

Lord. Here He comes. _____ Hold fast, help is on __ the way. Hold

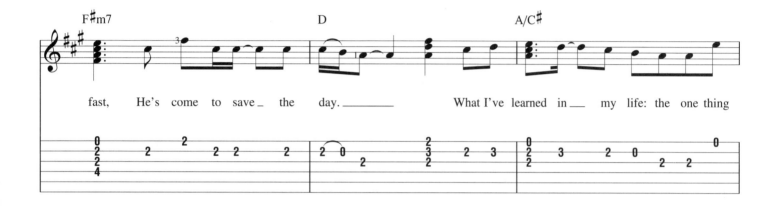

fast, He's come to save _ the day. _____ What I've learned in __ my life: the one thing

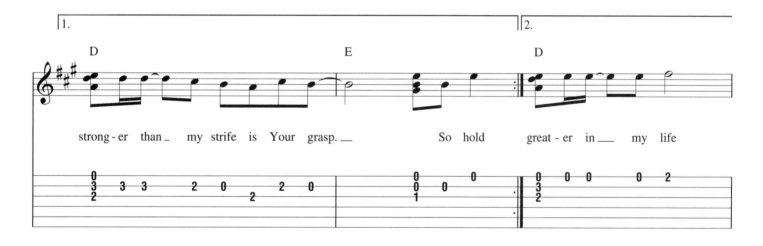

strong - er than _ my strife is Your grasp. _ So hold great - er in __ my life

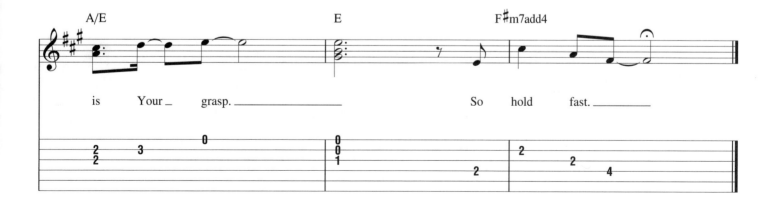

is Your _ grasp. _____ So hold fast. _____

Homesick

Words and Music by Bart Millard

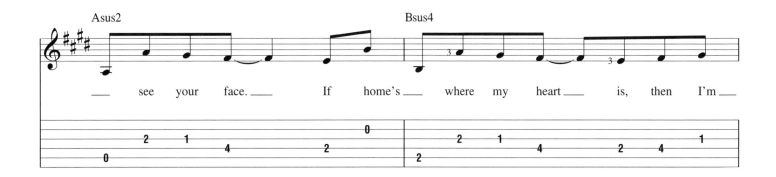

see your face. ___ If home's ___ where my heart ___ is, then I'm ___

___ out of place. ___ Lord, won't You give me strength _ to make it through _ some -

how? I've nev - er been more home - sick than now. ___

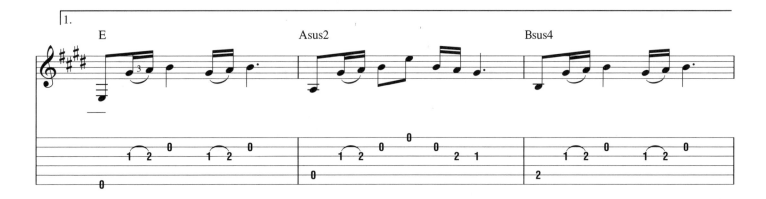

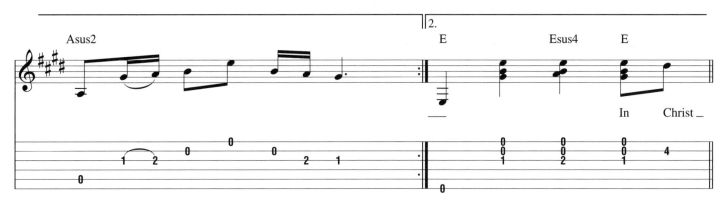

In Christ ___

Bridge

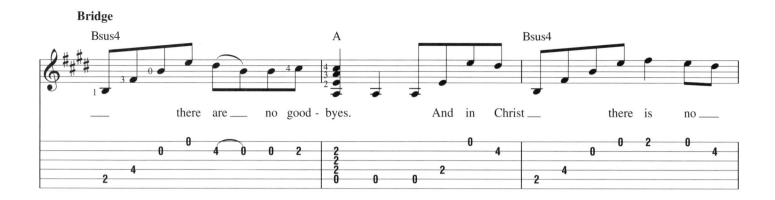

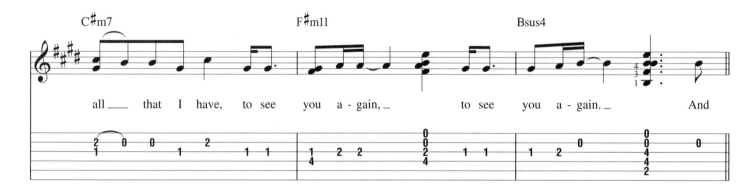

Chorus

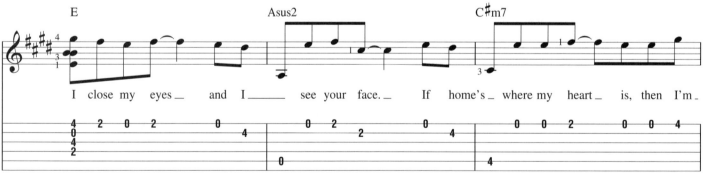

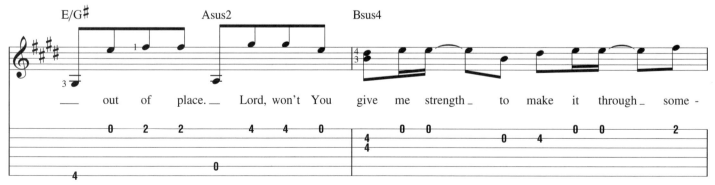

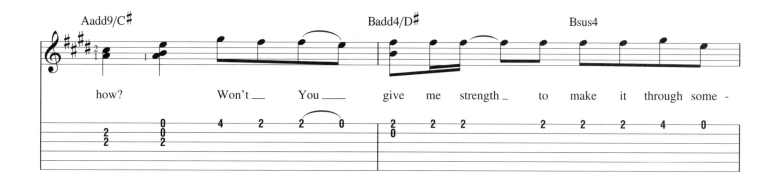

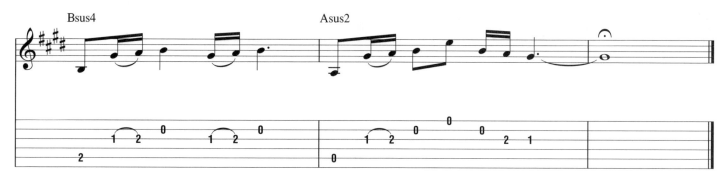

The Hurt and the Healer

Words and Music by Jim Bryson, Nathan Cochran, Bart Millard, Mike Scheuchzer, Robby Shaffer and Barry Graul

*Optional: To match recording, place capo at 2nd fret.

vain. You're all I have, __ all that re - mains. So here I am, what's
You. Lord, take hold __ and pull me through.

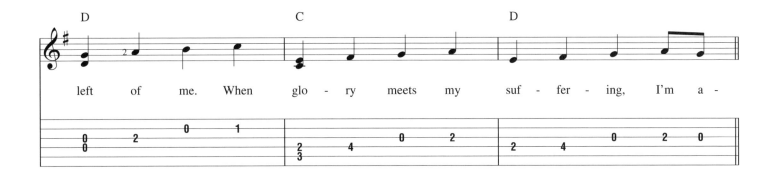

left of me. When glo - ry meets my suf - fer - ing, I'm a -

𝄋 Chorus

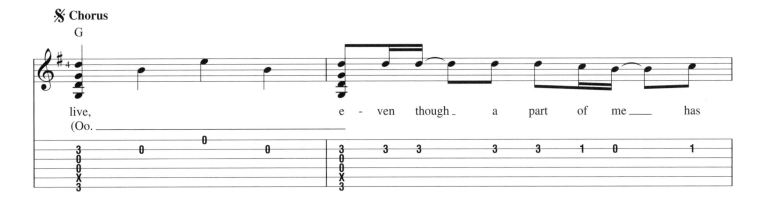

live, e - ven though __ a part of me __ has
(Oo. __

died. You take my heart __ and breathe it back __ to
Oo. __

life. I fall in - to __ Your arms o - pen wide when the
Oo.) __

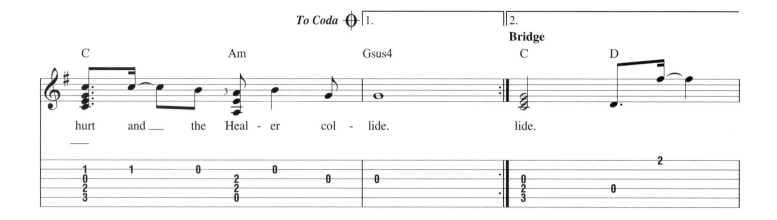

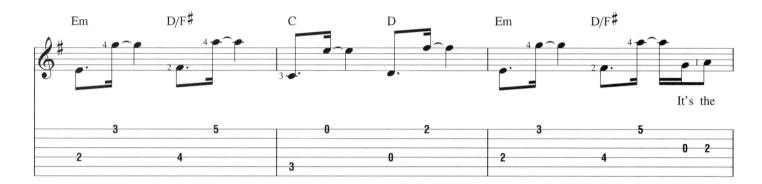

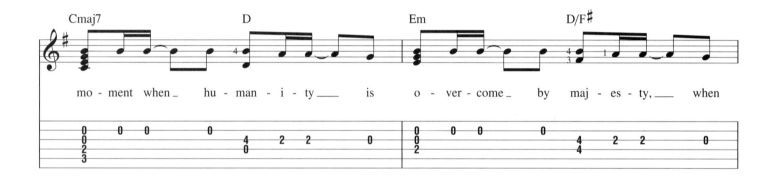

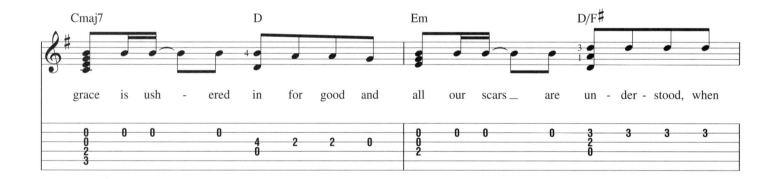

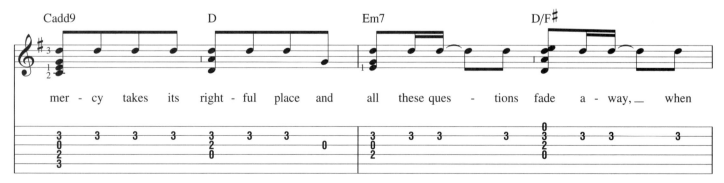

*Sung at once.

**Sung at once.

I Can Only Imagine

Words and Music by Bart Millard

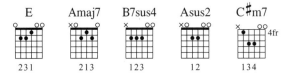

Strum Pattern: 1
Pick Pattern: 1

Intro
Moderately

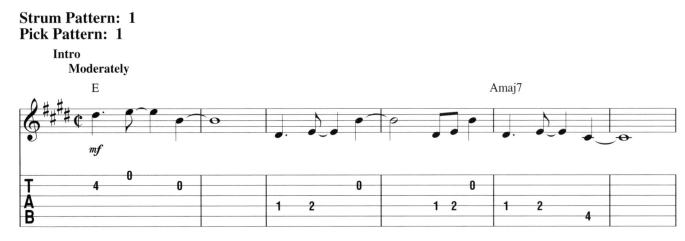

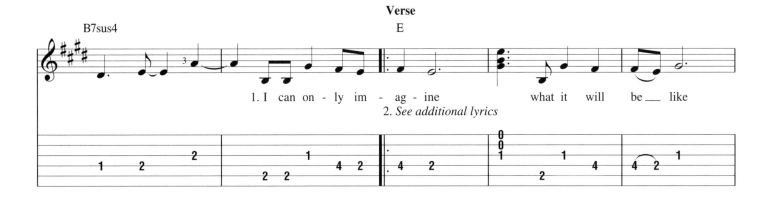

1. I can on - ly im - ag - ine what it will be ___ like
2. *See additional lyrics*

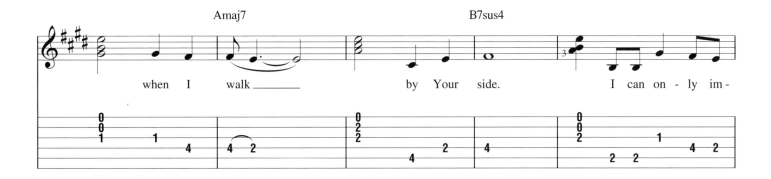

when I walk _____ by Your side. I can on - ly im-

ag - ine what my eyes will see when Your face _____

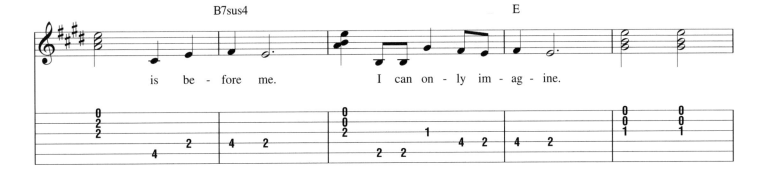

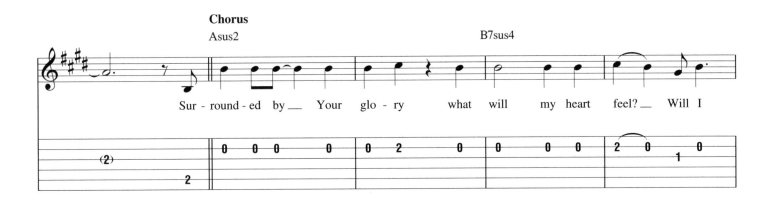

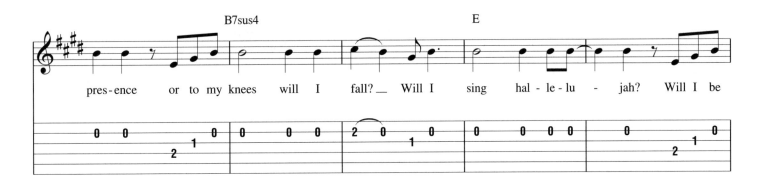

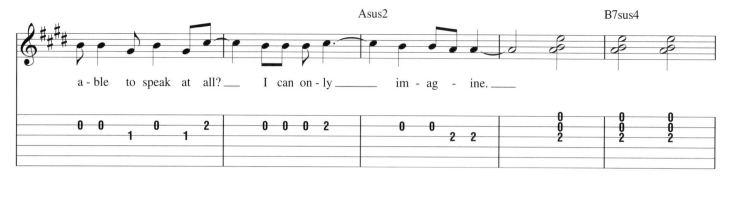

a - ble to speak at all?__ I can on - ly _____ im - ag - ine. __

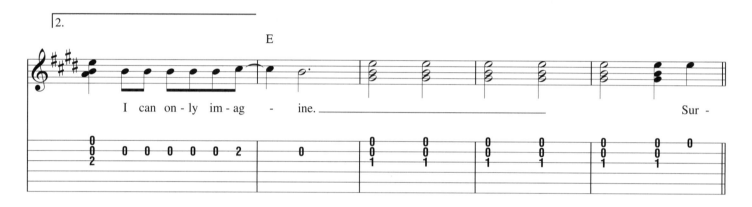

1.

I can on - ly im - ag - ine. __ 2. I can on - ly im-

2.

I can on - ly im - ag - ine. _____ Sur -

Chorus

round - ed by __ Your glo - ry, what will my heart feel? Will I dance for You, Je -

- sus, or in awe of You __ be still? Will I stand in Your pres - ence or to my

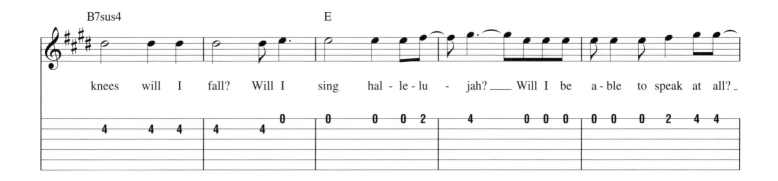

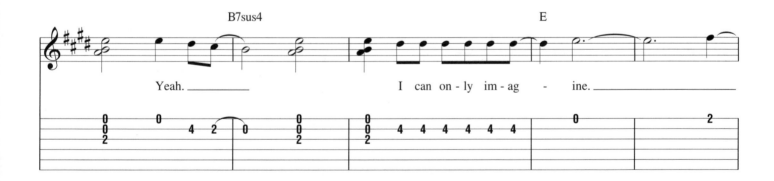

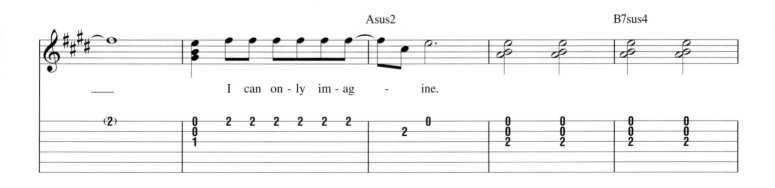

*Let chord ring, next 4 meas.

Outro

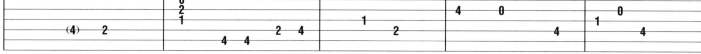

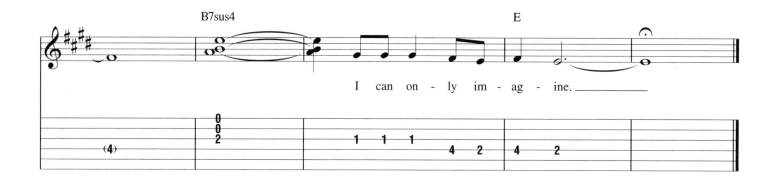

Additional Lyrics

2. I can only imagine when that day comes,
And I find myself standing in the Son.
I can only imagine when all I will do
Is forever, forever worship You.
I can only imagine.
I can only imagine.

Shake

Words and Music by Ben Glover, David Garcia, Solomon Olds and Bart Millard

*Optional: To match recording, place capo at 1st fret.

** ⊓ = down stroke, ∨ = up stroke.

*eyes

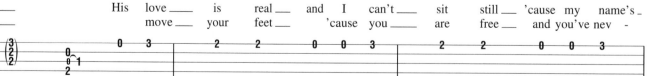

To Coda 1 ⊕

*more

**changed

***Lyrics in italics are shouted throughout.

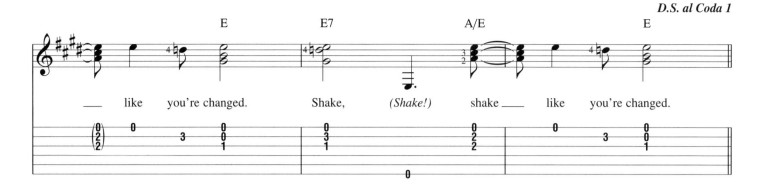

like you're changed. Shake, *(Shake!)* shake ___ like you're changed.

 Coda 1

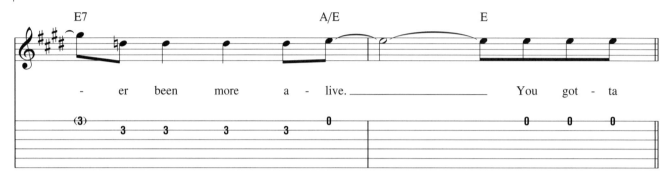

\- er been more a - live. ___ You got - ta

Chorus

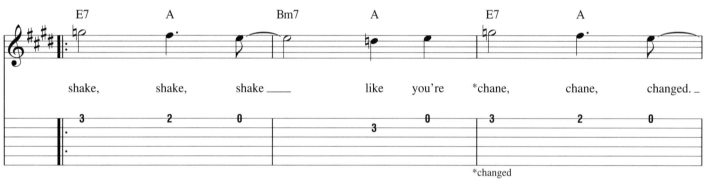

shake, shake, shake ___ like you're *chane, chane, changed. ___

*changed

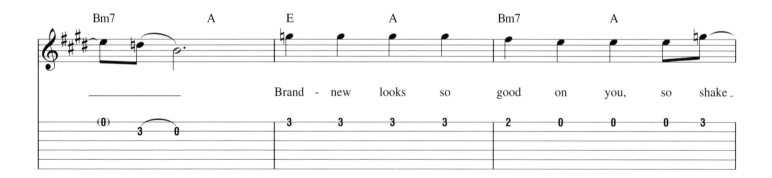

___ Brand - new looks so good on you, so shake ___

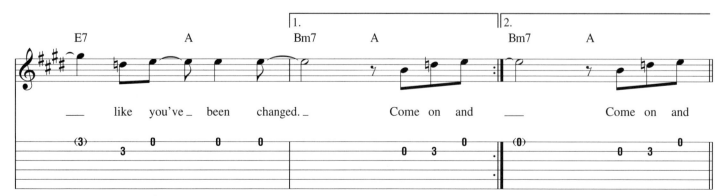

___ like you've ___ been changed. ___ Come on and ___ Come on and

In the Blink of an Eye

Words and Music by Bart Millard, Nathan Cochran, Mike Scheuchzer, Jim Bryson, Robby Shaffer, Barry Graul and Peter Kipley

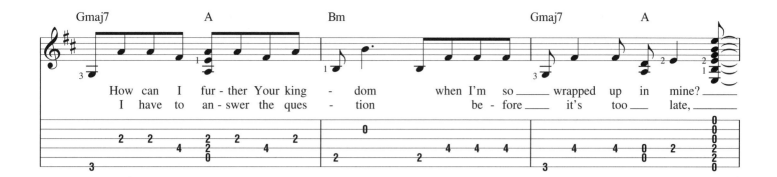

How can I fur - ther Your king - dom when I'm so ___ wrapped up in mine? ___
I have to an - swer the ques - tion be - fore ___ it's too ___ late, ___

Chorus

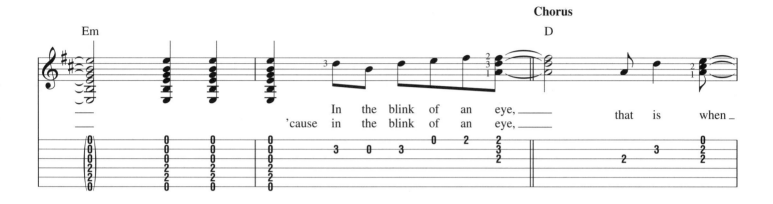

In the blink of an eye, ___ that is when ___
'cause in the blink of an eye, ___

___ I'll be clos - er to You ___ than I've ev - er been. Time will fly, ___

___ but un - til then ___ I'll em - brace ___ ev - 'ry mo - ment I'm giv -

1.

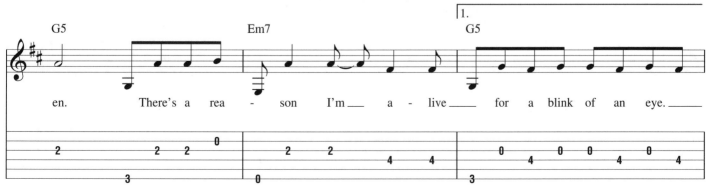

en. There's a rea - son I'm ___ a - live ___ for a blink of an eye. ___

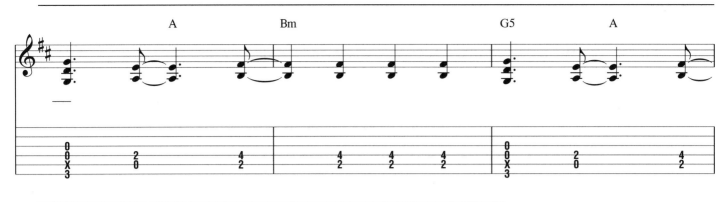

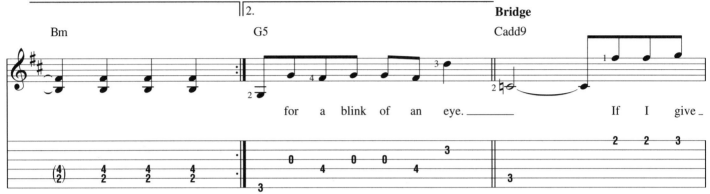

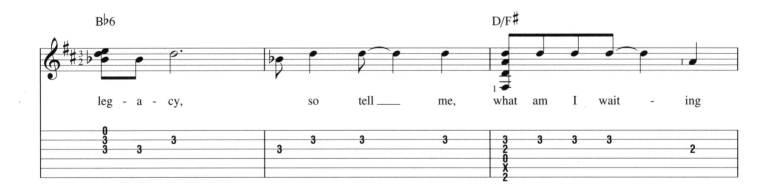

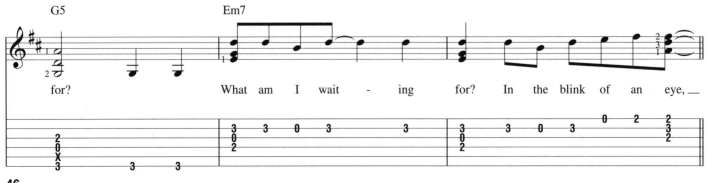

Chorus

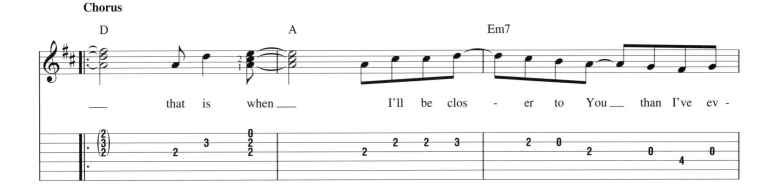

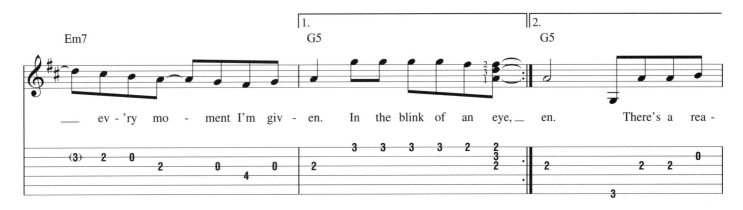

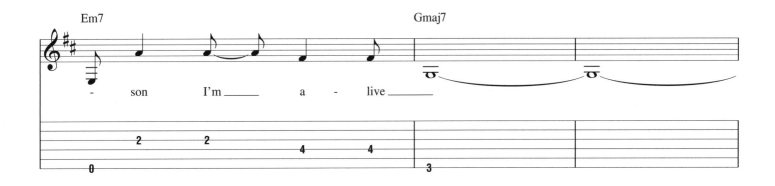

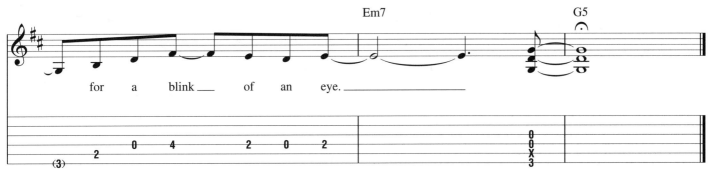

So Long Self

Words and Music by Bart Millard, Barry Graul, Jim Bryson, Nathan Cochran, Mike Scheuchzer and Robby Shaffer

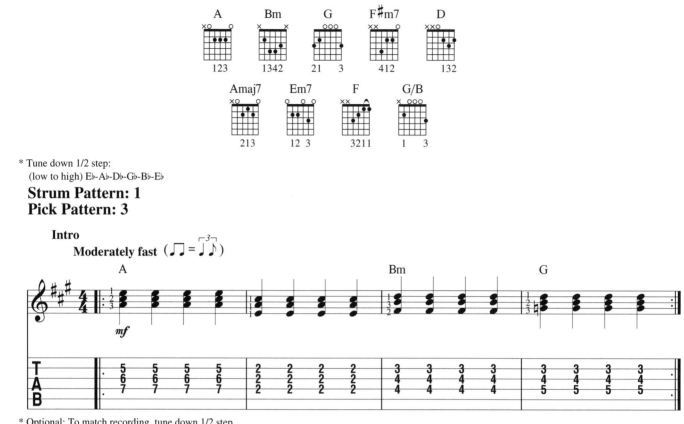

* Tune down 1/2 step:
(low to high) E♭-A♭-D♭-G♭-B♭-E♭

Strum Pattern: 1
Pick Pattern: 3

Intro

Moderately fast

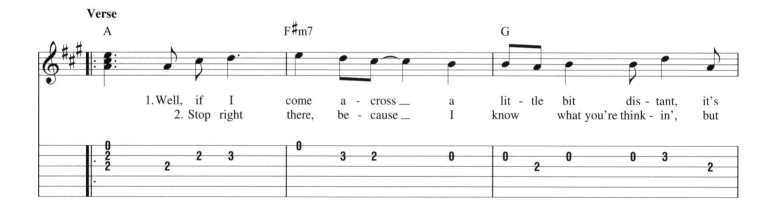

* Optional: To match recording, tune down 1/2 step.

Verse

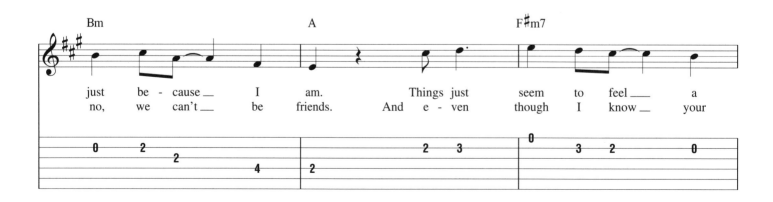

1. Well, if I come a - cross __ a lit - tle bit dis - tant, it's
2. Stop right there, be - cause __ I know what you're think - in', but

just be - cause __ I am. Things just seem to feel __ a
no, we can't __ be friends. And e - ven though I know __ your

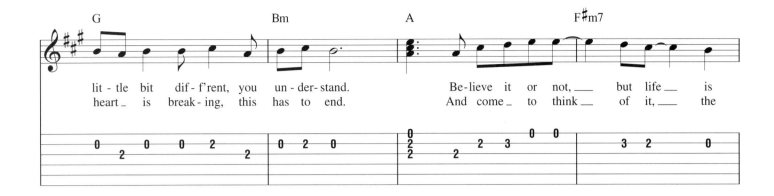

lit - tle bit dif - f'rent, you un - der - stand. Be - lieve it or not, ___ but life ___ is
heart ___ is break - ing, this has to end. And come ___ to think ___ of it, ___ the

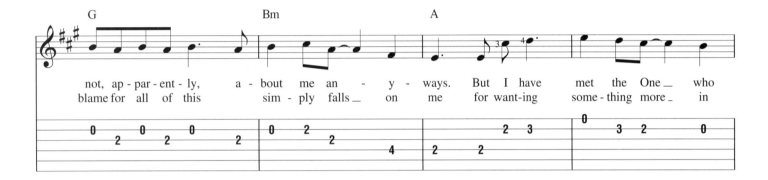

not, ap - par - ent - ly, a - bout me an - y - ways. But I have met the One ___ who
blame for all of this sim - ply falls ___ on me for want - ing some - thing more ___ in

𝄋 **Chorus**

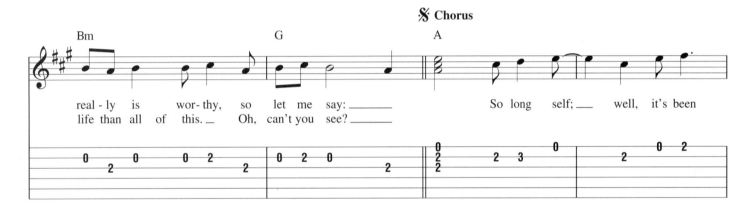

real - ly is wor - thy, so let me say: _____ So long self; ___ well, it's been
life than all of this. ___ Oh, can't you see? _____

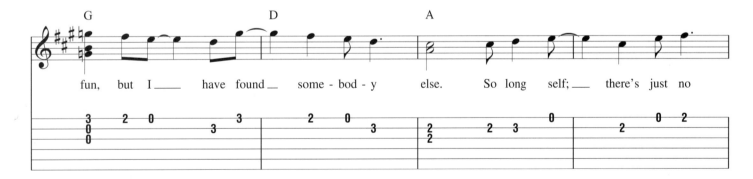

fun, but I ____ have found ___ some - bod - y else. So long self; ___ there's just no

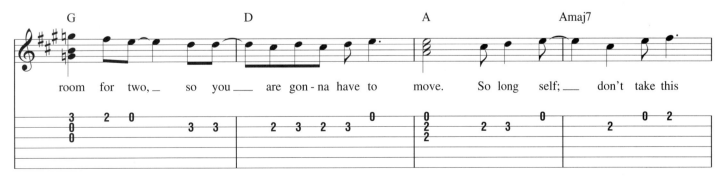

room for two, ___ so you ___ are gon - na have to move. So long self; ___ don't take this

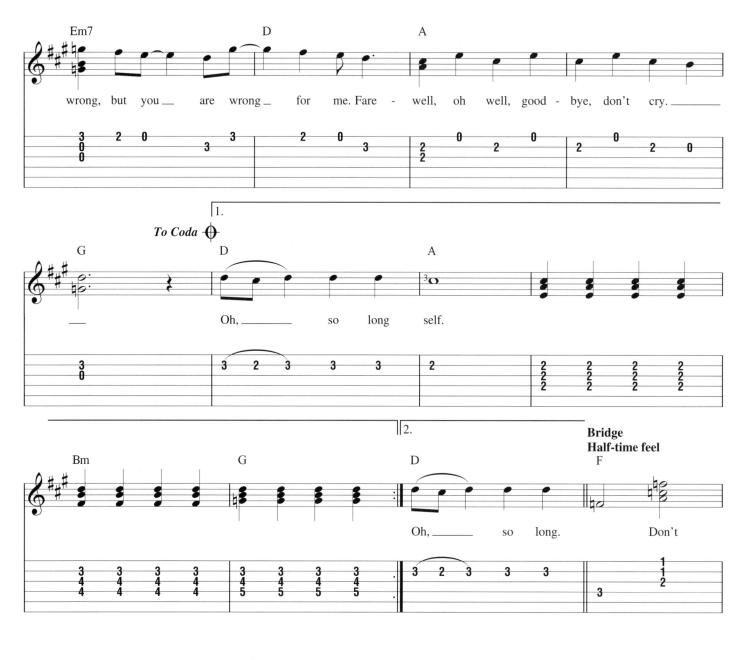

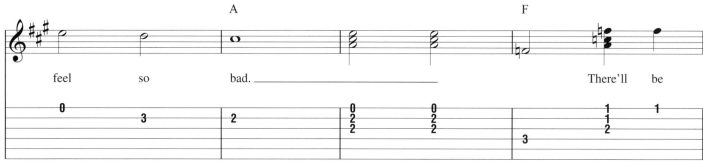

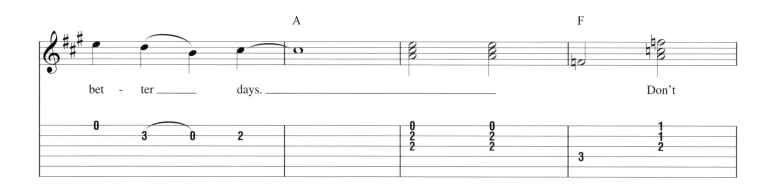

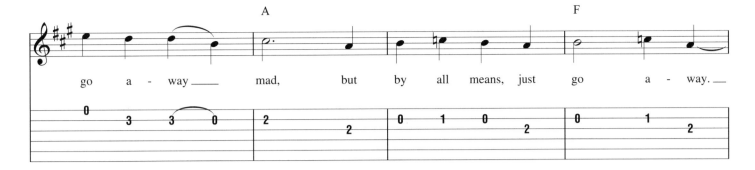

go a-way ___ mad, but by all means, just go a-way. ___

Interlude
End half-time feel

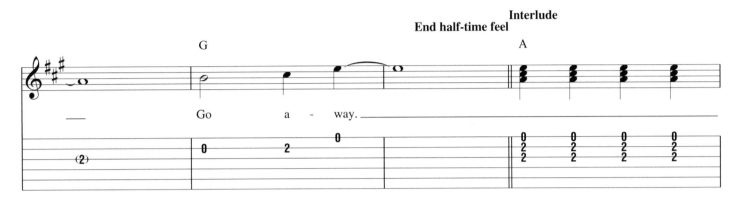

___ Go a-way. ___

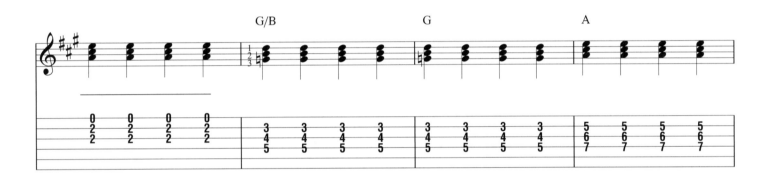

D.S. al Coda

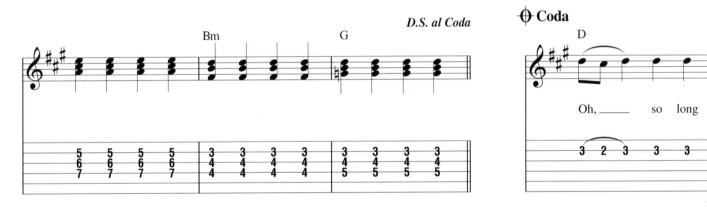

Oh, ___ so long

Outro

Repeat and fade

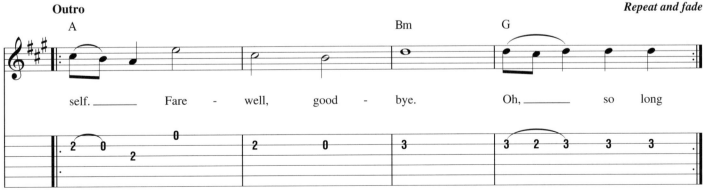

self. ___ Fare - well, good - bye. Oh, ___ so long

Spoken For

Words and Music by Bart Millard, Jim Bryson, Mike Scheuchzer, Nathan Cochran, Robby Shaffer and Pete Kipley

Chorus

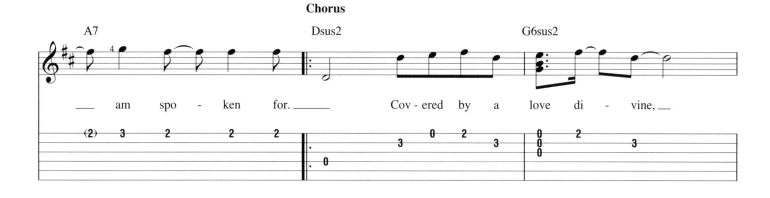

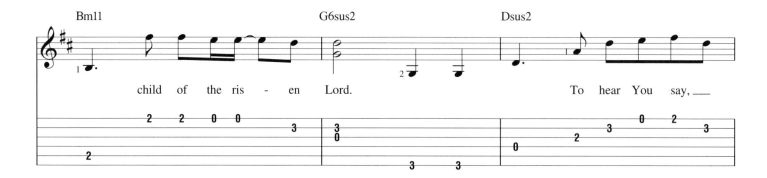

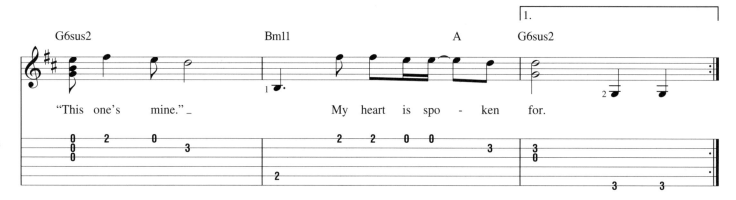

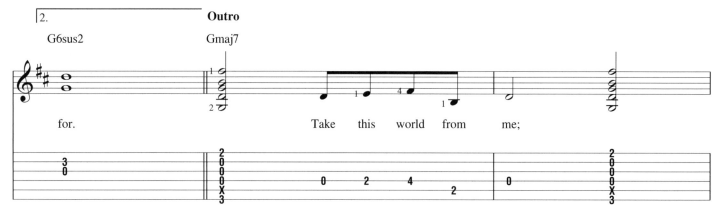

Outro

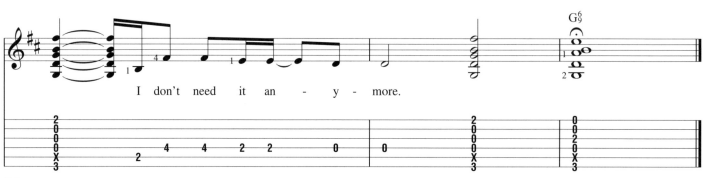

Word of God Speak

Words and Music by Bart Millard and Pete Kipley

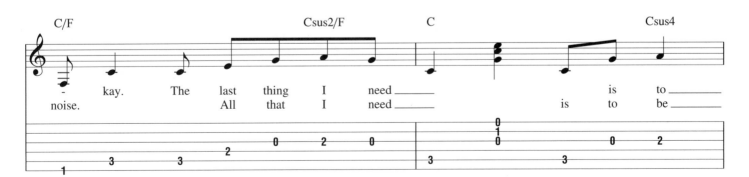

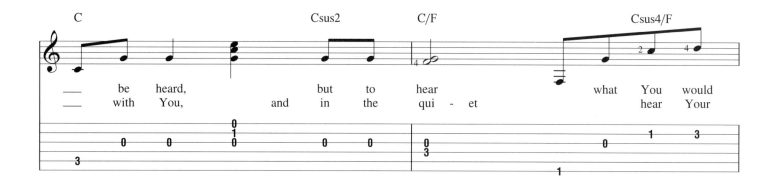

be heard, but to hear what You would
with You, and in the qui - et hear Your

𝄋 Chorus

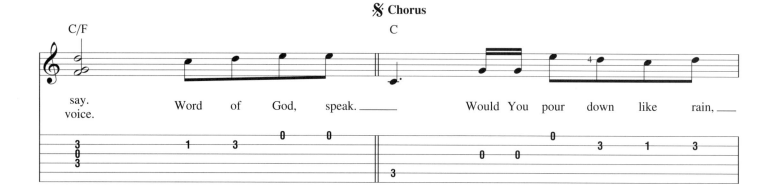

say. Word of God, speak. _____ Would You pour down like rain, ___
voice.

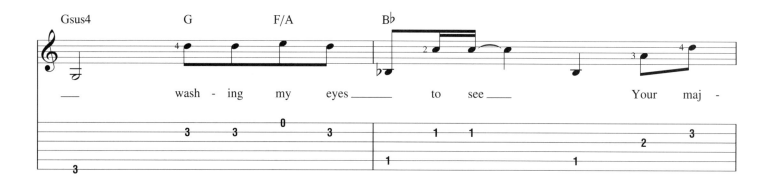

wash - ing my eyes _____ to see ___ Your maj -

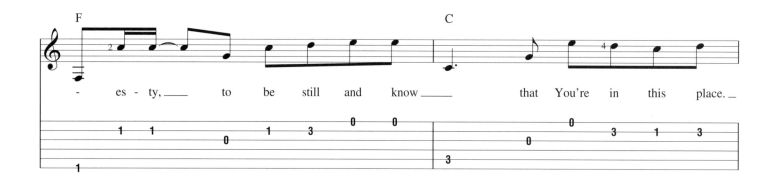

- es - ty, ___ to be still and know _____ that You're in this place. _

To Coda ⊕

___ Please let me stay _____ and rest ___ in Your ho -

You Are I Am

Words and Music by Jason Ingram, Dan Muckala, Barry Graul, Bart Millard,
Jim Bryson, Mike Scheuchzer, Nathan Cochran, Robby Shaffer and Seth Mosley

*Tune down 1/2 step:
(low to high) Eb-Ab-Db-Gb-Bb-Eb

Strum Pattern: 2
Pick Pattern: 2

*Optional: To match recording, tune down 1/2 step.

Interlude

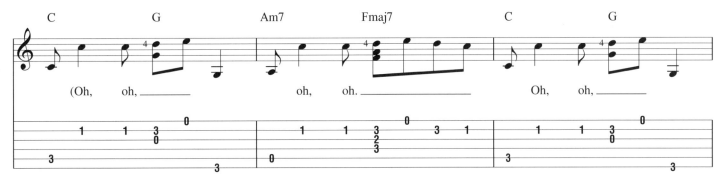

(Oh, oh, _____ oh, oh. _____ Oh, oh, _____

Verse

oh, oh.) _____

2. I've been the one ___ to try and say
3. I've been the one ___ held down in chains

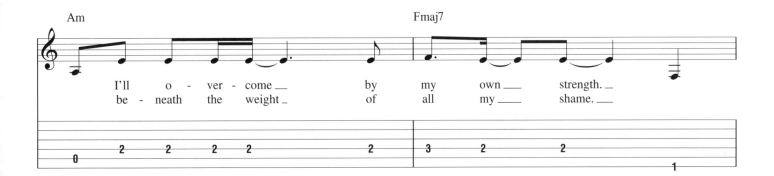

I'll o - ver - come ___ by my own ___ strength. ___
be - neath the weight ___ of all my ___ shame. ___

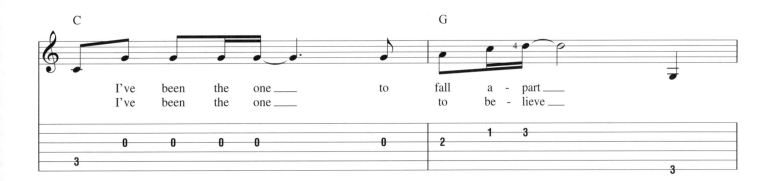

I've been the one _____ to fall a - part ___
I've been the one _____ to be - lieve ___

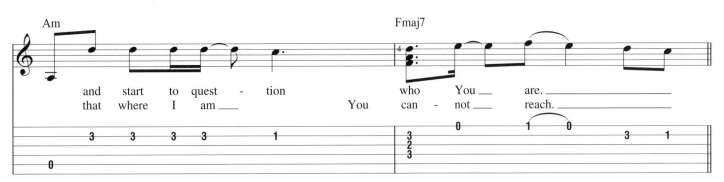

and start to ques - tion who You ___ are. _____
that where I am ___ You can - not ___ reach. _____

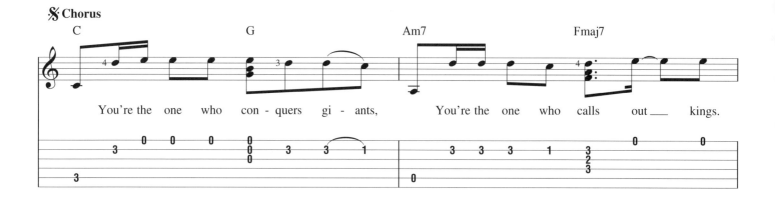

You're the one who con-quers gi-ants, You're the one who calls out ___ kings.

You shut the mouths of li-ons, You tell the dead to ___ breathe.

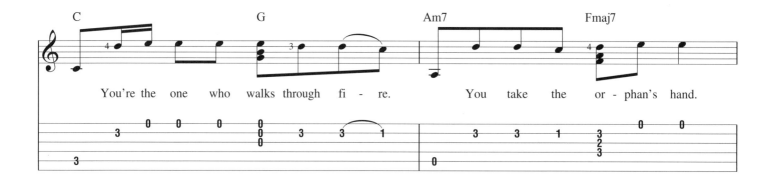

You're the one who walks through fi-re. You take the or-phan's hand.

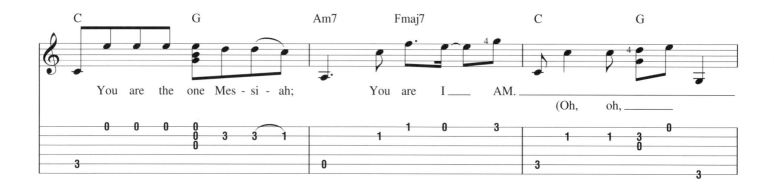

You are the one Mes-si-ah; You are I ___ AM. ___ (Oh, oh, ___

3rd time, To Coda ⊕

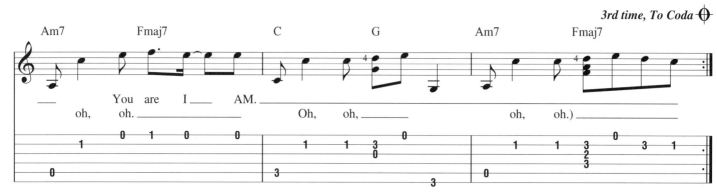

___ You are I ___ AM. oh, oh. Oh, oh, oh, oh.)

The veil is torn and now I live

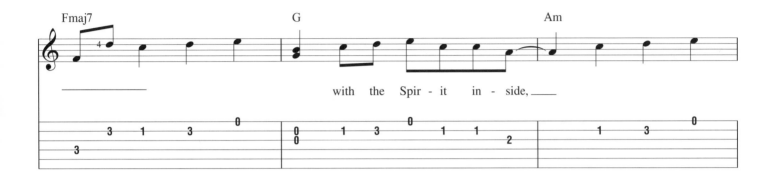

with the Spir - it in - side,

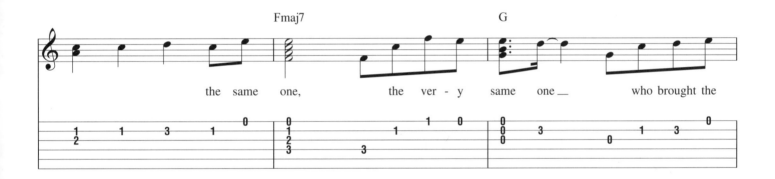

the same one, the ver - y same one who brought the

Son back to life. Hal - le - lu - jah, He

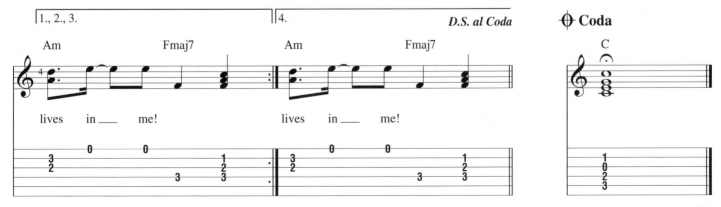

lives in me! lives in me!

christian**guitar**songbooks

 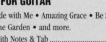

EASY GUITAR WITH NOTES & TAB

This series features simplified arrangements with notes, tab, chord charts, and strum and pick patterns.

MIXED FOLIOS

00702287	Acoustic	$14.99
00702002	Acoustic Rock Hits for Easy Guitar	$12.95
00702166	All-Time Best Guitar Collection	$19.99
00699665	Beatles Best	$12.95
00702232	Best Acoustic Songs for Easy Guitar	$12.99
00702233	Best Hard Rock Songs	$14.99
00703055	The Big Book of Nursery Rhymes & Children's Songs	$14.99
00322179	The Big Easy Book of Classic Rock Guitar	$24.95
00698978	Big Christmas Collection	$16.95
00702394	Bluegrass Songs for Easy Guitar	$12.99
00703387	Celtic Classics	$14.99
00118314	Chart Hits of 2012-2013	$14.99
00702149	Children's Christian Songbook	$7.95
00702237	Christian Acoustic Favorites	$12.95
00702028	Christmas Classics	$7.95
00101779	Christmas Guitar	$14.99
00702185	Christmas Hits	$9.95
00702016	Classic Blues for Easy Guitar	$12.95
00702141	Classic Rock	$8.95
00702203	CMT's 100 Greatest Country Songs	$27.95
00702283	The Contemporary Christian Collection	$16.99
00702006	Contemporary Christian Favorites	$9.95
00702239	Country Classics for Easy Guitar	$19.99
00702282	Country Hits of 2009–2010	$14.99
00702240	Country Hits of 2007–2008	$12.95
00702225	Country Hits of '06–'07	$12.95
00702085	Disney Movie Hits	$12.95
00702257	Easy Acoustic Guitar Songs	$14.99
00702280	Easy Guitar Tab White Pages	$29.99
00702212	Essential Christmas	$9.95
00702041	Favorite Hymns for Easy Guitar	$9.95
00702281	4 Chord Rock	$9.99
00702286	Glee	$16.99
00699374	Gospel Favorites	$14.95
00702160	The Great American Country Songbook	$15.99
00702050	Great Classical Themes for Easy Guitar	$6.95
00702116	Greatest Hymns for Guitar	$8.95
00702130	The Groovy Years	$9.95
00702184	Guitar Instrumentals	$9.95
00702046	Hits of the '70s for Easy Guitar	$8.95
00702273	Irish Songs	$12.99
00702275	Jazz Favorites for Easy Guitar	$14.99
00702274	Jazz Standards for Easy Guitar	$14.99
00702162	Jumbo Easy Guitar Songbook	$19.95
00702258	Legends of Rock	$14.99
00702261	Modern Worship Hits	$14.99
00702189	MTV's 100 Greatest Pop Songs	$24.95
00702272	1950s Rock	$14.99
00702271	1960s Rock	$14.99
00702270	1970s Rock	$14.99
00702269	1980s Rock	$14.99
00702268	1990s Rock	$14.99
00109725	Once	$14.99
00702187	Selections from O Brother Where Art Thou?	$12.95
00702178	100 Songs for Kids	$12.95
00702515	Pirates of the Caribbean	$12.99
00702125	Praise and Worship for Guitar	$9.95
00702155	Rock Hits for Guitar	$9.95
00702285	Southern Rock Hits	$12.99
00702866	Theme Music	$12.99
00121535	30 Easy Celtic Guitar Solos	$14.99
00702124	Today's Christian Rock – 2nd Edition	$9.95
00702220	Today's Country Hits	$9.95
00702198	Today's Hits for Guitar	$9.95
00702217	Top Christian Hits	$12.95
00702235	Top Christian Hits of '07–'08	$14.95
00103626	Top Hits of 2012	$14.99
00702294	Top Worship Hits	$14.99
00702206	Very Best of Rock	$9.95
00702255	VH1's 100 Greatest Hard Rock Songs	$27.99
00702175	VH1's 100 Greatest Songs of Rock and Roll	$24.95
00702253	Wicked	$12.99

ARTIST COLLECTIONS

00702267	AC/DC for Easy Guitar	$15.99
00702598	Adele for Easy Guitar	$14.99
00702001	Best of Aerosmith	$16.95
00702040	Best of the Allman Brothers	$14.99
00702865	J.S. Bach for Easy Guitar	$12.99
00702169	Best of The Beach Boys	$12.99
00702292	The Beatles — 1	$19.99
00702201	The Essential Black Sabbath	$12.95
00702140	Best of Brooks & Dunn	$10.95
02501615	Zac Brown Band — The Foundation	$16.99
02501621	Zac Brown Band — You Get What You Give	$16.99
00702095	Best of Mariah Carey	$12.95
00702043	Best of Johnny Cash	$16.99
00702033	Best of Steven Curtis Chapman	$14.95
00702291	Very Best of Coldplay	$12.99
00702263	Best of Casting Crowns	$12.99
00702090	Eric Clapton's Best	$10.95
00702086	Eric Clapton — from the Album Unplugged	$10.95
00702202	The Essential Eric Clapton	$12.95
00702250	blink-182 — Greatest Hits	$12.99
00702053	Best of Patsy Cline	$10.95
00702229	The Very Best of Creedence Clearwater Revival	$14.99
00702145	Best of Jim Croce	$12.99
00702278	Crosby, Stills & Nash	$12.99
00702219	David Crowder*Band Collection	$12.95
00702122	The Doors for Easy Guitar	$12.99
00702276	Fleetwood Mac — Easy Guitar Collection	$12.99
00702190	Best of Pat Green	$19.95
00702136	Best of Merle Haggard	$12.99
00702243	Hannah Montana	$14.95
00702227	Jimi Hendrix — Smash Hits	$14.99
00702288	Best of Hillsong United	$12.99
00702236	Best of Antonio Carlos Jobim	$12.95
00702245	Elton John — Greatest Hits 1970–2002	$14.99
00702204	Robert Johnson	$9.95
00702277	Best of Jonas Brothers	$14.99
00702234	Selections from Toby Keith — 35 Biggest Hits	$12.95
00702003	Kiss	$9.95
00702193	Best of Jennifer Knapp	$12.95
00702216	Lynyrd Skynyrd	$15.99
00702182	The Essential Bob Marley	$12.95
00702346	Bruno Mars — Doo-Wops & Hooligans	$12.99
00702248	Paul McCartney — All the Best	$14.99
00702129	Songs of Sarah McLachlan	$12.95
02501316	Metallica — Death Magnetic	$15.95
00702209	Steve Miller Band — Young Hearts (Greatest Hits)	$12.95
00702096	Best of Nirvana	$14.95
00702211	The Offspring — Greatest Hits	$12.95
00702030	Best of Roy Orbison	$12.95
00702144	Best of Ozzy Osbourne	$14.99
00702279	Tom Petty	$12.99
00102911	Pink Floyd	$16.99
00702139	Elvis Country Favorites	$9.95
00702293	The Very Best of Prince	$12.99
00699415	Best of Queen for Guitar	$14.99
00109279	Best of R.E.M.	$14.99
00702208	Red Hot Chili Peppers — Greatest Hits	$12.95
00702093	Rolling Stones Collection	$17.95
00702092	Best of the Rolling Stones	$14.99
00702196	Best of Bob Seger	$12.95
00702252	Frank Sinatra — Nothing But the Best	$12.99
00702010	Best of Rod Stewart	$14.95
00702049	Best of George Strait	$12.95
00702259	Taylor Swift for Easy Guitar	$14.99
00702260	Taylor Swift – Fearless	$12.99
00115960	Taylor Swift — Red	$16.99
00702290	Taylor Swift — Speak Now	$14.99
00702223	Chris Tomlin — Arriving	$12.95
00702262	Chris Tomlin Collection	$14.99
00702226	Chris Tomlin — See the Morning	$12.95
00702427	U2 — 18 Singles	$14.99
00702108	Best of Stevie Ray Vaughan	$10.95
00702123	Best of Hank Williams	$12.99
00702111	Stevie Wonder — Guitar Collection	$9.95
00702228	Neil Young — Greatest Hits	$15.99
00119133	Neil Young – Harvest	$14.99
00702188	Essential ZZ Top	$10.95

Prices, contents and availability subject to change without notice.

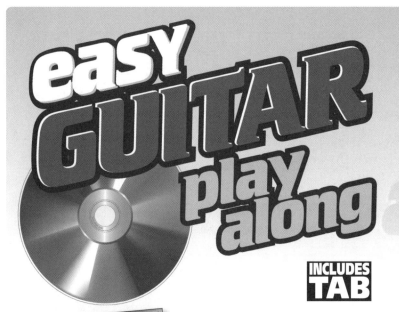

easy GUITAR play along

The *easy GUITAR play along*® Series features streamlined transcriptions of your favorite songs. Just follow the tab, listen to the CD to hear how the guitar should sound, and then play along using the backing tracks. The CD is playable on any CD player, and is also enhanced to include the Amazing Slowdowner technology so Mac and PC users can adjust the recording to any tempo without changing the pitch!

INCLUDES TAB

1. ROCK CLASSICS
Jailbreak • Living After Midnight • Mississippi Queen • Rocks Off • Runnin' Down a Dream • Smoke on the Water • Strutter • Up Around the Bend.

00702560 Book/CD Pack....... $14.99

2. ACOUSTIC TOP HITS
About a Girl • I'm Yours • The Lazy Song • The Scientist • 21 Guns • Upside Down • What I Got • Wonderwall.

00702569 Book/CD Pack....... $14.99

3. ROCK HITS
All the Small Things • Best of You • Brain Stew (The Godzilla Remix) • Californication • Island in the Sun • Plush • Smells like Teen Spirit • Use Somebody.

00702570 Book/CD Pack....... $14.99

4. ROCK 'N' ROLL
Blue Suede Shoes • I Get Around • I'm a Believer • Jailhouse Rock • Oh, Pretty Woman • Peggy Sue • Runaway • Wake up Little Susie.

00702572 Book/CD Pack........ $14.99

5. ULTIMATE ACOUSTIC
Against the Wind • Babe, I'm Gonna Leave You • Come Monday • Free Fallin' • Give a Little Bit • Have You Ever Seen the Rain? • New Kid in Town • We Can Work It Out.

00702573 Book/CD Pack........ $14.99

6. CHRISTMAS SONGS
Have Yourself a Merry Little Christmas • A Holly Jolly Christmas • The Little Drummer Boy • Run Rudolph Run • Santa Claus Is Comin' to Town • Silver and Gold • Sleigh Ride • Winter Wonderland.

00101879 Book/CD Pack......... $14.99

7. BLUES SONGS FOR BEGINNERS
Come On (Part 1) • Double Trouble • Gangster of Love • I'm Ready • Let Me Love You Baby • Mary Had a Little Lamb • San-Ho-Zay • T-Bone Shuffle.

00103235 Book/CD Pack..... $14.99

8. ACOUSTIC SONGS FOR BEGINNERS
Barely Breathing • Drive • Everlong • Good Riddance (Time of Your Life) • Hallelujah • Hey There Delilah • Lake of Fire • Photograph.

00103240 Book/CD Pack..... $14.99

9. ROCK SONGS FOR BEGINNERS
Are You Gonna Be My Girl • Buddy Holly • Everybody Hurts • In Bloom • Otherside • The Rock Show • Santa Monica • When I Come Around.

00103255 Book/CD Pack..... $14.99

HAL•LEONARD®
CORPORATION
7777 W. BLUEMOUND RD. P.O. BOX 13819
MILWAUKEE, WISCONSIN 53213

Prices, contents, and availability subject to change without notice.

www.halleonard.com

0113